Genre Expository

Essential Question
How do people make government work?

The Race *for the* Presidency

by **Mary Atkinson**

Introduction

Have you ever voted for a class president? If so, you probably know that students choose between two or more classmates. These people are the candidates. They want people to vote for them. They hang up posters. They give speeches. They promise to do good things if they win. On election day, the one with the most votes wins.

Kelly Ca was a 12th grade class president when she introduced President Obama before he gave a speech in 2010.

The elections for the president of the United States are a bit like class elections. But they take much more time. Presidential elections are held every four years. The race for the presidency starts more than a year before the election.

WHO CAN BE PRESIDENT?

The president must:

★ be at least 35 years old

★ be a natural born U.S. citizen

★ have lived in the U.S. for 14 or more years.

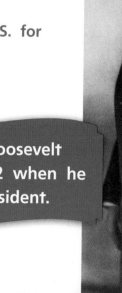

Theodore Roosevelt was only 42 when he became president.

Chapter 1

The Primary Campaign

The race for the presidency starts with special elections. These are called **primary elections**. Most candidates are part of a political party. In the United States, the two main parties are the Democrats and the Republicans. Voters choose candidates from each party to go on to the general election.

Some candidates stay **independent**. They do not belong to a party.

THE TWO MAIN PARTIES

The Democratic Party has been around since 1828. It aims to give all workers equal opportunities and justice.

★ The Republican Party was started in 1854. The first Republicans were against slavery. Today, the party aims to protect peoples' rights.

Each state has a primary election to pick the Republican candidate and the Democratic candidate they like. A few states don't hold primaries. The parties choose their candidates at a meeting called a **caucus**.

Democratic candidate Hillary Clinton talks to people outside a polling place in 2008.

During the primaries, the candidates try to convince people in their party to vote for them. They meet voters and talk about what they would do as president. Voters read newspapers and watch TV to figure out whom to vote for.

Voters go to a polling place to cast their vote.

The two main parties each hold meetings after the primaries. These meetings are called conventions. Each party announces a candidate for president and vice president. There are speeches and parties. They talk about their ideas. They plan their **campaign**.

STOP AND CHECK

What are the primaries?

The candidates for president and vice president are chosen at conventions.

Chapter 2

The General Election

After the conventions, the final campaigns begin. The Republican candidate and the Democratic candidate travel around the country. They want to convince as many people as they can to vote for them. Many people work for each campaign. They plan events and raise money.

2004 candidate John Kerry met the public as part of his campaign.

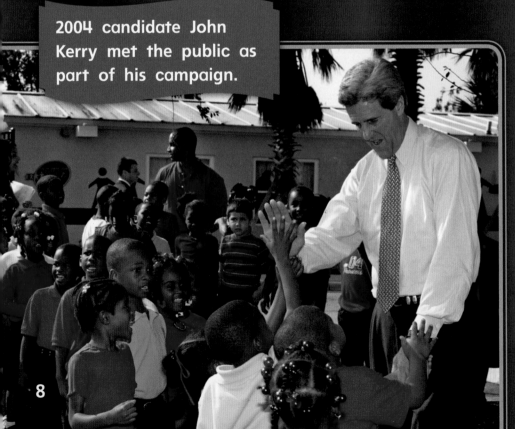

(t) Photodisc/Punchstock, (b) Kerry-Edwards 2004, Inc./Sharon Farmer, photographer

To win the election, the candidates need to know what kind of government people want. Candidates talk to people to find out their problems. They do research. They ask questions and collect the answers.

CAMPAIGNS IN THE PAST

Candidates in the past couldn't zip across the country in planes or talk on television. They got noticed in other ways. Cross-country train journeys, known as whistle-stop tours, were popular.

Candidates make promises about what they will do. Reporters and voters ask the candidates hard questions. They want to find out if the candidates' ideas will work. They want to know if there will be any problems if they elect a candidate.

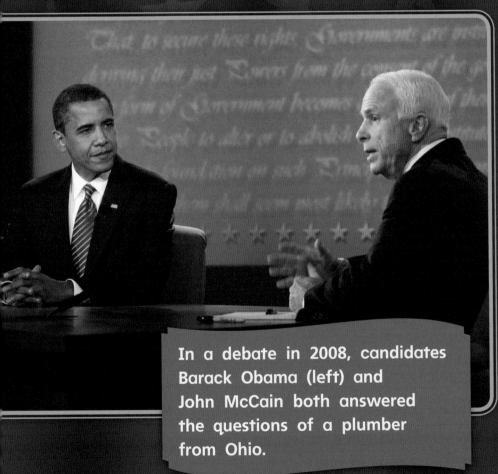

In a debate in 2008, candidates Barack Obama (left) and John McCain both answered the questions of a plumber from Ohio.

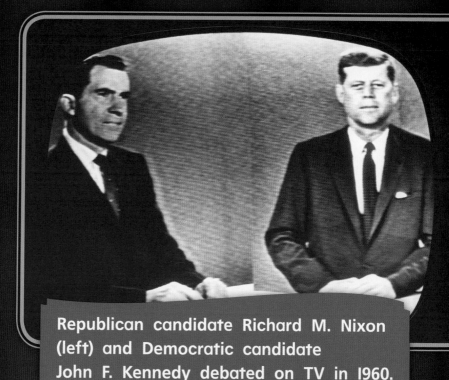

Republican candidate Richard M. Nixon (left) and Democratic candidate John F. Kennedy debated on TV in 1960.

Debates are a good way to find out about candidates. The two candidates explain their own policies. They find mistakes in each other's policies. The debates are shown on TV. They can be exciting to watch. Most importantly, they help voters make a decision about how to vote.

STOP AND CHECK

What do candidates do during a debate?

11

Chapter 3

Election Day

Election day is the first Tuesday after the first Monday in November. Polling places are set up. Poll workers help voters. They make sure the election is fair.

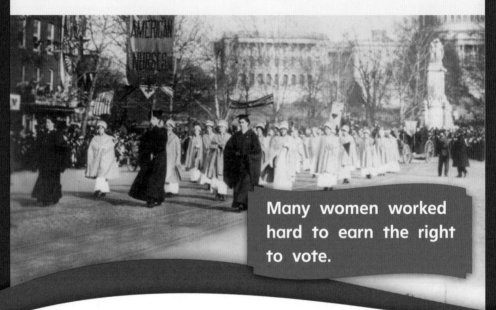

Many women worked hard to earn the right to vote.

(t) Photodisc/Punchstock, (b) Library of Congress, Prints and Photographs Division (LC-USZ62-35138)

VOTING TIME LINE

1856	1870
All white men over the age of 21 have the right to vote.	African American men age 21 or older gain the right to vote.

Election day is exciting. Who will win? The results for each state are shown on TV. People estimate the final vote. Maps show which states gain a Democratic win and which gain a Republican win. Finally the winners are announced.

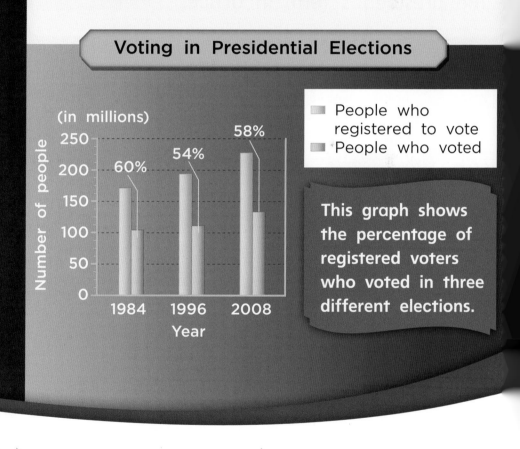

Voting in Presidential Elections

(in millions)

Number of people

People who registered to vote
People who voted

58%
54%
60%

1984   1996   2008
Year

This graph shows the percentage of registered voters who voted in three different elections.

1920	Today
Women age 21 or older gain the right to vote.	Most U.S. citizens age 18 or older have voting rights.

It is usually on January 20 that the new or reelected president is sworn in. This day is known as Inauguration Day. The ceremony takes place at the U.S. Capitol in Washington, D.C. It is the beginning of the president's term in office.

On January 20, 2009, Barack Obama took the Oath of Office. He became the 44th President of the United States.

(t) Photodisc/Punchstock, (b) Noah K. Murray/Star Ledger/CORBIS

STOP AND CHECK

What happens on election day?

Respond to Reading

Summarize

Use details from *The Race for the Presidency* to summarize the selection. Your graphic organizer may help you.

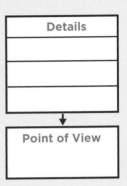

Text Evidence

1. How do you know that *The Race for the Presidency* is expository text? Genre

2. What is the author's point of view about election day? Author's Point of View

3. What does the word *reelected* on page 14 mean? Prefixes

4. Use details from the text to write about why the author thinks the candidate debates are important.

Write About Reading

Compare Texts
Read about how students changed a law.

Elementary School
Lawmakers

In 2006 a group of third- and fourth-graders wanted to change the law. The students wanted to make the pumpkin the official state fruit of New Hampshire. They had found out that pumpkins grew throughout the state.

Franz-Marc Frei/CORBIS

Every October the people of Keene, New Hampshire, hold a pumpkin festival.

Peter Allen was a state representative. He had liked the students' research. He had put up a bill asking that the pumpkin become the state fruit. The students had spoken in support of their idea.

The class had reached out to other students. They asked them to send postcards supporting the bill. In March, their bill had passed the House vote. In April, it needed to pass the Senate vote.

VEGETABLE OR FRUIT?

Is a pumpkin a fruit or a vegetable? A fruit is the part of the plant with seeds. A vegetable is any other part of a plant that we eat. Pumpkins contain pumpkin seeds, so they are fruits.

Senator Robert Boyce wanted the strawberry to be the state fruit. The students were unsure which way the vote would go. Finally, the senators voted. They voted twenty-three to one for the pumpkin. The students had become lawmakers.

NEW HAMPSHIRE LAW

CHAPTER 3: STATE EMBLEMS, FLAG, ETC.

Section 3:24 State Fruit.

3:24 State Fruit. – The pumpkin is hereby designated as the official state fruit of New Hampshire.

Make Connections

Do people know what the result will be when they vote for a bill? Essential Question

What do presidential candidates do to get votes? Did the students do the same things to get people to vote for the pumpkin? Text to Text

Glossary

campaign *(kam-PAYN)* a set of activities to help get somebody elected *(page 7)*

caucus *(KAW-kus)* a meeting to choose candidates that is only open to members of the party *(page 5)*

debates *(duh-BAYTS)* organized discussions between people *(page 11)*

independent *(in-duh-PEN-duhnt)* a person who does not belong to any party *(page 4)*

primary elections *(PRIGH-me-ree i-LEK-shunz)* elections for party members to choose candidates *(page 4)*

Index

Focus on
Social Studies

Purpose To see how surveys can be used for campaigning.

What to Do

Step 1 Make a list of colors (or fruits, or some other item). Ask each person to choose their favorite.

Step 2 Write the number of people that chose each item.

Step 3 Make a "Vote for..." poster for the second most popular item.

Step 4 Have a vote between the first and second most popular items.

Conclusion Which item did you think would be the most popular? How did your ideas change?